Eddie Murphy

by Teresa Koenig
& Rivian Bell

Lerner Publications Company
Minneapolis

LIBRARY OF CONGRESS CATALOGING IN PUBLICATION DATA

Koenig, Teresa.
    Eddie Murphy.

    Summary: Describes how black comedian Eddie Murphy rose from class clown to television and film star.
    1. Murphy, Eddie — Juvenile literature. 2. Comedians — United States — Biography — Juvenile literature.
3. Entertainers — United States — Biography — Juvenile literature. [1. Murphy, Eddie. 2. Comedians.
3. Entertainers. 4. Afro-Americans — Biography. I. Bell, Rivian. II. Title.
PN2287.M815K63   1985 792.7′028′0924 [B] [92] 84-29696
ISBN 0-8225-1602-0 (lib. bdg.)

    2   3   4   5   6   7   8   9   10   94   93   92   91   90   89   88   87   86   85

Contents

The World of Eddie Murphy

"Ed-die! Ed-die! Ed-die!" chants the crowd in a downtown Washington, D.C., record store. The store is jammed with enthusiastic fans straining to catch a glimpse of a remarkable young comedian named Eddie Murphy. He enters the store and flashes his famous ear-to-ear grin, and everyone cheers.

Eddie has come to autograph his award-winning album "Eddie Murphy: Comedian." He jokes and laughs with the people who have waited in line for hours to meet him. It is clear that Eddie Murphy makes people feel good. "All I'm out to do is to make people laugh," he says, and he usually succeeds.

Eddie frequently appears on "The Tonight Show" to discuss his current projects with Johnny Carson.

After two hours of signing autographs, Eddie leaves for another meeting in another city. Before the day ends, he will have visited two radio stations and will have flown to New York for a late-night television appearance.

Sometimes making people laugh can be hard work. But for Eddie Murphy, it is all he has ever wanted to do. When Eddie was only 15 years old, he told his mother he wanted to be famous by the time he turned 19. He kept his promise and took his talents into nightclubs and to television, records, and motion pictures. He is a comedian, a serious actor, a musician, and a singer-songwriter. It seems there is nothing he cannot do.

How <u>does</u> Eddie Murphy do it?

Eddie in the Early Years

Laughter and a sense of humor have always been important to Eddie Murphy. As a young boy, his family used to encourage him to see the funny side of life, even when it wasn't easy to do so.

Born April 3, 1961, in Brooklyn, New York, Eddie Murphy was the younger son of Charles and Lillian Murphy. Charles, a policeman for the New York Transit Authority, and Lillian, a telephone operator, separated when Eddie was three years old. Soon after the separation, his mother became

nd Eddie and his brother Charles were
ster home. They were raised for a short
voman who was not as loving as their
"These were baaaad days," he remem-
thinks that those difficult times were
⌐vably the reason I became a comedian."

When Eddie's mother recovered, she married a
man named Vernon Lynch. Eddie and Charles were
once again able to live at home with their mother
and stepfather in the town of Roosevelt, Long
Island, near New York City. It was here that Eddie
began to use his special sense of humor. First at
home and later at school, he discovered he could
make people laugh.

One day when Eddie was in the third grade, his
teacher offered an ice-cream pie to the student
who could tell the best story. Right then, Eddie
made up a funny story, and he won the pie. In the
tradition of many other comedians, he became the
class clown, and his talent grew from there.

When he wasn't in school, Eddie watched television, which gave him many ideas about how to
be funny. He studied and perfected impressions of
the cartoon characters Tom and Jerry and Bugs
Bunny. "You'd never be sitting around with just
Eddie," his mother recalled, "but always with some
other character."

Eddie remembered a lot about the people and

10

characters he watched on television, and soon he could imitate practically anyone. His early favorites were Bruce Lee, the Beatles, and Elvis Presley. As Eddie grew older, he discovered two black comedians, Bill Cosby and Richard Pryor, who became his idols. Later in his comedy career, Eddie would credit Richard Pryor for having influenced him more than any other comedian had.

It was not long before Eddie began developing comedy routines of his own. He would disappear into the basement of his house for hours just to practice his jokes. His worried mother would call down to him to make sure he was all right, and Eddie would just tell her, "I'm rehearsing!" His mother was not certain what he meant, but she knew he had talent and left him alone. Eddie's parents encouraged Eddie and made sure their home was filled with love and understanding for each of their children. They earned his loyalty, his love, and his respect.

When Eddie reached his 15th birthday, he felt ready to stop rehearsing and start performing. He started by serving as master of ceremonies for the Roosevelt Youth Center talent show. He had a chance to perform about five minutes of his own material and then imitated Richard Pryor's routine for the rest of the show. Eddie gladly worked for free—he was finally up on a real stage! He realized,

"Looking out at the audience, I knew that I was in show business for the rest of my life."

The important thing Eddie learned from this first job was that he needed to practice more in front of different types of audiences. He worked harder at writing his own comedy routines, and he slowly improved his joke and storytelling skills and his confidence on stage. For a year, Eddie performed free at a club called The White House Inn. When he felt ready, he moved on to other clubs where he could perform for as much as $25 a show. Before long, he was performing regularly at important comedy clubs in New York City, such as the Improvisation and the Comic Strip.

Eddie worked harder on his jokes than he did on his high-school homework. His grades dropped so low in the tenth grade that he was forced to repeat a year. "I don't want to tell you what that did to me," he said. "I went to summer school, I doubled up on classes, and I graduated only a couple of months late."

Eddie Murphy graduated from Roosevelt High School in the summer of 1979. His classmates voted him the most popular boy in the class, and everyone who knew him at Roosevelt High felt he would be successful. Underneath his picture in the school yearbook he wrote, "Future plans: Comedian."

That prediction came true sooner than anyone, except Eddie, would have expected. Just out of high school, Eddie had found two important managers to help him with his career. When the chance to try out for the popular television comedy show "Saturday Night Live" came along, he was ready. The producers tested Eddie six times before hiring him as a featured player. He was not yet a regular cast member, but he did earn $750 a week—more than he had ever earned. Eddie was on his way!

A Saturday Night Star

The producers and audience of "Saturday Night Live" soon became aware of Eddie's star quality. When Eddie first appeared with his new friend, TV star Joe Piscopo, the two comedians held the spotlight of the show. They enacted a story about a school that refused to let whites on the basketball team. Eddie came out on stage to explain the difference between blacks and whites. He held up a large "boom box" radio and said, "If God created us equal, why didn't he give you one of these?"

The laughter that followed proved that a real talent was at work. The rest of that season was a disaster, however, because the producer was inexperienced and the rest of the cast did not see comedy in the same way that Eddie and Joe Piscopo did. When NBC hired a new producer for the 1981-82 season, he kept only two cast members, Joe and Eddie, and promoted Eddie to regular-cast status. He also raised Eddie's salary to $4,500 per show.

By the third show of the season, the producer was convinced that Eddie was the reason for the show's success. In one interview, he called Eddie "the comic of the 80's. He and Chevy Chase are the only two people this show's ever had who could talk to a camera like it was a person." Eddie got along well with the rest of the cast, in part because he was a nice person to work with, and also because he was just plain talented, and they knew it.

Eddie's popularity began to skyrocket. He became known not only for the remarkable way he could imitate such stars as Stevie Wonder, Bill Cosby, and Mr. T, but also for special characters he created. Audiences came to love his Gumby and his Buckwheat from the rerun series "The Little Rascals." Eddie also created Mister Robinson, a man who resembled the kindly Mister Rogers of

Eddie and the cast welcome Steve Martin to "Saturday Night Live."

the children's TV show, and Raheem Abdul Muhammed, who reminded many viewers of Muhammed Ali.

Every week, Eddie was given at least one and sometimes three solo spots for which he wrote all of his own material. On the show's script, the staff writers would simply write "Eddie" to indicate that the rest of the writing was up to him.

By now audiences were flocking to television sets on Saturday nights just to see Eddie perform. Many people tried to understand why viewers found Eddie's kind of comedy so enjoyable. One critic called it his charm, while his producer said it was the charm in Eddie's eyes. "His eyes tell the audience he's laughing," he explained.

Eddie later tried to explain his own brand of humor. "My comedy is good-time comedy," he told a reporter for *Rolling Stone* magazine. "Conversations and fooling around with my friends, stuff that just happened to me. That's why I poke fun at everybody, 'cause I'm just out there. It's comedy."

Eddie is quick to point out that, while he is black, he is not an angry black performer, but rather a performer with a black point of view. Eddie isn't interested in making the audience hostile, but in creating comedy from characters that are *real.*

One example of Eddie's "real" characters is an old black man he created for his "Solomon and Pudge" routines. The idea came from a skit he used to do with his good friend, Clinton Smith, about two blues musicians. Eddie's old man character is down on his luck but too proud to show it. The character is real to Eddie, and it's also his favorite of all the television characters he's ever created.

By the time Eddie was 21, he was an accomplished television star earning a great deal of money. Surprisingly, he was still living at home, although he did finally move to his own apartment that year. He picked one only a few minutes from his family so that he could stay near his mother.

Even though he was a star, Eddie stayed close to his family and tried to arrange his schedule so that he could pick his mother up when she finished working. "My family's happiness is the most important thing to me," he said. And he proved it with the many gifts he gave his mother, father, and brother.

He also bought a few things for himself. "You're only going to be 21 once," he said. "I don't drink or do drugs, but I run around a lot. I like cars and jewelry—rings and necklaces, nothing too gaudy." Eddie became known not only for his funny skits but also for his red and black leather outfits, gold jewelry, and cool sunglasses.

Eddie was also offered more than just a large salary for appearing on "Saturday Night Live." He was offered a contract to make an album of his live comedy act, which he recorded at the Comic Strip in New York. He appeared on "The Tonight Show," and he signed to do a comedy special for cable television. But most important, Eddie was offered a role in his first motion picture. This was the beginning for Eddie Murphy, actor.

Eddie Murphy on Screen

Eddie got his chance in a peculiar way. He'd had plenty of movie offers, but none that he and his managers felt was right. Then his idol, Richard Pryor, dropped out of a movie called *48 Hrs.* in which he had been scheduled to star. The filming was supposed to begin right after the close of the television season. Eddie took Pryor's part and signed on for $200,000 to play the black convict released for 48 hours to help a white city detective locate a killer and his sidekick.

Co-stars Nick Nolte and Eddie Murphy team up to track down a cop killer and his accomplice in _48 Hrs_.

The film's Reggie Hammond character suited Eddie perfectly. In fact, Eddie rewrote part of the script to give Reggie more personality. He even changed the name to Reggie from Willie Biggs. Eddie described Reggie as "a real hip character: articulate, wears Armani suits, and drives a Porsche. You've never seen a black thief portrayed that way."

Eddie played opposite a well-known film star, Nick Nolte, who portrayed Detective Jack Cates. While their characters were very different (the white detective was tough and ready to fight, while the black thief was smooth-talking and well mannered), Eddie and Nick shared a lot during their filming together. They met every morning in makeup to discuss how they would act together when the cameras rolled.

The film was released in time for the 1982 Christmas season and was considered a success from its first day at the box office. Reviews were good, and the picture earned more than $80 million in ticket sales alone. One newspaper critic said, "Murphy livens up *48 Hrs.* the minute he struts into view. He is so instantly likable that, although he never looks tough enough to have survived so much as a minute in prison, he has the audience cheering him on . . ."

Being in the movies was one of the biggest thrills of Eddie's life. He told a *Rolling Stone* reporter about the first time he saw *48 Hrs.* "It was a sneak preview, and I snuck into the theater. They showed my name on the screen, and the audience *clapped.* I was on cloud nine for two weeks."

By coincidence, his first movie hit the box office at the same time he began his second film, *Trading Places.* Paramount Studios, who made *48 Hrs.*, were so pleased with Eddie's work they rushed him a special contract and a cool $1 million just to make sure he would work with them again!

Teamed with former "Saturday Night Live" star Dan Aykroyd, Eddie had become a full-fledged star. Dan and Eddie played the parts of two men who couldn't be more different: Dan was the wealthy investment broker Louis Winthrope II, while Eddie played Billy Ray Valentine, a con man who used his wits to survive. The scheme that brings the two men together is dreamed up by two greedy old bankers from Philadelphia, who try a test. They set out to prove that, with enough money and the right job, Billy Ray can be as cultured as Louis, and Louis will be as crooked as Billy Ray. They trick the two men into trading places. Before the movie is over, Louis and Billy Ray uncover the plot and trap the two old men in their own scheme.

Eddie and Dan began filming in Philadelphia on December 13, 1982. They soon found themselves surrounded by admirers, who tried to stop them for autographs. Filming continued in New York, where the appearance of the two stars almost created a business disaster. The producers planned to film one scene using real Wall Street brokers during a regular day of trading. But when Eddie and Dan came out, all the brokers stopped working to stare at the stars and cheer them on.

Trading Places became the hit of the 1983 summer season. It opened at 1,368 theaters across the country and took in $30 million in its first three weeks. The movie stayed in the top ten that entire summer as critic after critic hailed the picture's success.

Ophelia (Jamie Lee Curtis) helps Billy Ray (Eddie) and Louis (Dan Aykroyd) plot their revenge in *Trading Places*.

In *Beverly Hills Cop,* Judge Reinhold plays Detective Billy Rosewood, a naive Beverly Hills detective whose assignment is to trail Axel Foley (Eddie) and make sure he doesn't create any disturbances in ritzy Beverly Hills. But Axel, fresh from Detroit, can't seem to stay out of trouble and charms Billy into helping him hunt down his best friend's killers.

26

Eddie wasted no time and immediately began rehearsing for a starring role in another Paramount movie, *Beverly Hills Cop*. In it, Eddie plays the part of a tough cop who leaves the streets of Detroit for the beauty of Beverly Hills to investigate the murder of a friend. The movie was completed in time for the 1984 Christmas season.

While Eddie was delighted with the public's warm response to his acting ability, Paramount studios was even happier. They offered Eddie an almost unheard-of contract: a chance to star in five movies, and a chance to produce the films as well. All this for $15 million.

The Future Eddie Murphy

That movie contract would be enough for most young stars, but not for Eddie. While his movies were playing to cheering audiences, he kept busy doing another season of "Saturday Night Live" and released two award-winning albums. His first album, "Eddie Murphy," was nominated for two Grammy awards. His second album, "Eddie Murphy: Comedian," quickly sold a million copies, and this time he won a Grammy for Best Comedy Recording of the year.

But Eddie wanted to try his creative talents in other areas as well. In April 1984, CBS Records released Eddie's first pop single, "Party All the Time." Eddie recorded the song with help from his good friend Rick James, the recording star. Eddie clearly enjoys singing and has a style all his own.

To keep up his musical interests, Eddie has set up a studio in his new home in Alpine, New Jersey. In the privacy of his own home, he can try his hand at songwriting and recording with the help of a drum set, guitar, bass, electric piano, synthesizer, and rhythm machine. In fact, that's just about the only "furniture" in Eddie's house! Eddie plays all the instruments himself. Elvis Presley is Eddie's musical idol. "He's the greatest entertainer who ever lived," Eddie believes.

Some people think Eddie Murphy deserves the title "greatest entertainer" himself. A talented comedian, movie actor, and now singer, there doesn't seem to be much that he can't handle when there's a stage nearby. For all the fame and money he's acquired, however, Eddie still knows how important friends can be. While he likes all girls, he's decided to spend most of his time with just one, a student at a New York university. Eddie believes being with Lisa Figueroa keeps him from being too crazy. They plan to get married.

Eddie still pays a great deal of attention to his

family and friends. Whenever possible, he tries to hire his four or five closest friends to work with him, because they trust each other. He also wants to help them the way they helped him before he became famous.

If Eddie Murphy's past is any clue, he will be a talent for many years to come. He plans to make at least five more movies and a concert film, and he may record a pop album of his own songs. It's a big future for a young man who has never quit believing in himself. And still, he's modest. "There's a million guys out there like me. I was just fortunate. I was in the right place at the right time and said the right thing."

Luck, talent, and an ability to make people laugh —that's the Eddie Murphy formula for success.

Eddie backstage with some of his fans

Photo Credits

Mark Reinstein/Photoreporters, p. 4
Allan S. Adler/Photoreporters, p. 6
Geoffrey Croft/Retna, p. 8
James Colburn/Photoreporters, p. 14
Gary Gershoff/Retna, p. 17
Paramount Pictures, pp. 20 & 26
Photoreporters, p. 22
Wide World Photos, p. 25
Scott Alonzo/Retna, p. 28
John Bellissimo/Retna, p. 32

Front cover photo by Phil Roach/Photoreporters
Back cover photo by Geoffrey Croft/Retna